WOYZECK

by
Georg Büchner

translated & adapted by
Zach Trebino

Copyright © 2011 by Zach Trebino

All Rights Reserved

No part of this book may be reproduced, for any reason and by any means, without the express written permission of the publisher.

CAUTION: This play-text is fully protected, in whole, in part, or in any form under the copyright laws of the United States of America and all other countries of the Copyright Union, and is subject to royalty. All rights, including professional, amateur, educational, motion picture, radio, television, recitation, and public reading, among others, are strictly reserved. All injuries concerning use of this text should be addressed to Zach Trebino via e-mail at zachtrebino@gmail.com

ISBN: 9798643083412

First Edition.

Production History

The initial production of this translation/adaptation was produced by Homunculus, Inc with the help of George and Anna Condo. It was performed at Crane Arts, LLC as part of the 2011 Philadelphia International Fringe Festival. The production had the following team:

```
WOYZECK..........................................Paul Bayley
MARIE...........................................Louisa DeButts
THE CAPTAIN....................................Eleonore Condo
THE DOCTOR.........Sara Newman & Samantha Turret
THE DRUM MAJOR.........................John Wentworth
THE SERGEANT.........................Patrick McTamany
ANDRES................................................Matthew Austin
MARGARET.............................................Jessica Joy
MOTHER...................................................Maren Lord
THE BARKER.....................................Jared Fleischman
APPRENTICE #1................................Madison Ferris
APPRENTICE #2.............................Kayla Weinerman
THE MONKEY........................................Patrick Scheid
SOLDIERS, MEDICAL STUDENTS,
AND DRINKERS...................................Taylor Crist,
     Jared Fleishman, Patrick McTamany, & Patrick Scheid


DIRECTION........................................Zach Trebino
LIGHTS.................................................Ryan Killeen
ENVIRONMENT..............................Emily Baldasarra
SOUND...............................................Zach Trebino
COSTUMES & MAKEUP....................Angela Palaggi
```

Characters

    Franz Woyzeck
    Marie
    The Captain
    The Doctor
    The Drum Major
    The Sergeant
    Andres
    Margaret
    Mother
    The Barker
    Apprentice #1
    Apprentice #2
    The Monkey
    The Donkey
    Soldiers
    Medical Students
    Drinkers

Note on casting:
All of the roles in this adaptation are gender neutral. The script occasionally uses gendered pronouns, but that doesn't really mean all that much. It's, at best, a suggestion of some archetypical, ineffable stage presence rather than an actual gender identity. Any production can choose to have specifically gendered actors play specifically gendered characters, even if the character's gender does not match that of the actor, or a production could embrace genderlessness across the board.

Note on the set:
This adaptation works best with a fluid, almost boundary-less unit set. It can be performed in proscenium, of course, but that's boring and inhumane. It's best done in a 3/4 thrust or an alley stage. The set should be anchored on one end by a water element - be it a kiddie pool, a fish tank, or a pond - and on the other end by some modular mound of detritus - that becomes Marie's room and a spinning barber's chair for the Captain to sit in as Woyzeck shaves them, among other things.

Note on the 'Scene Transitions':
The author has taken the liberty of including scene transitions. These are, of course, not proscriptive. They serve to illustrate the connection and interactivity among all the play's characters - like gas molecules sealed in a slowly heating heating bell jar or nodes in a blockchain. Do with them what you will.

PROLOGUE

As the audience waits to enter the theatre, WOYZECK, ANDRES, THE SERGEANT, THE CAPTAIN, and THE DRUM MAJOR intrude upon the waiting area, performing a square bashing routine led by THE CAPTAIN. It is an arduous and brutal display of military exercises - for which WOYZECK is unrepentantly browbeat and THE DRUM MAJOR is deified. This carries on for some time - 10, 20 minutes.

I.

The BARKER emerges from the theatre and blows a horn; their pet MONKEY runs to their heel. The CAPTAIN orders the soldiers to cease their square bashing.

By now, the rest of the actors, in their various characters, are among the waiting audience too, having been joining the crowd for some time now. MARIE finds WOYZECK and runs to him as his blind MOTHER and the CHILD dance their way through the crowd.

MOTHER
(singing)
Just like us, the Earth won't last
Oh how soon this all will pass
Life itself is passing gas
A little stink that flees so fast

WOYZECK
Ha ha! Oh, my poor old Mum. It's all sorrow till it's joy. Hello my young child! Hello Marie. Shall I carry you?

BARKER
Great honored guests! The well-to-do and the ne'er-do-wells! Lend me your rears!

MARIE
(indicating the BARKER)
If we let fools talk sense once in a awhile, soon enough they'll be the only ones talking. What a mad world!

WOYZECK
What a beautiful world.

BARKER
(showcasing their pet monkey)
Observe god's marvelous creature. It's a nothing! A mere nothing. Yet look at what it's achieved with a little culture! It can walk on two feet, carry a sword, whistle a tune while wiping its own ass! Yes, indeed, this monkey is a soldier. Though that's not saying much, no it's not. They are the *lowest* form of humanity after all - soldiers. Now, my little army man, bow to us! Give us a kiss!

The MONKEY farts. The CROWD jeers and cheers.

BARKER
He's a musical asshole, isn't it? Folks, in here you'll see the cosmic donkey - the great ass of Being! And all the favored spiders of the crowned heads of Europe. The mystic muskrat who'll tell you everything - how old your kids are, what your grandmother had for her last meal! All the links in the great chain of being! Come! Come! The performance is now! If we're ever to end, the beginning must begin!

WOYZECK
Should we head in?

MARIE
It might be too nice for us. Look at that man's pants! And her shoes!

WOYZECK

Nonsense. Nothing too good for my loves!

> *WOYZECK escorts MARIE, the CHILD, and his MOTHER into the theatre as the DRUM MAJOR and the SERGEANT watch.*

DRUM MAJOR
(to the Sergeant, pointing to MARIE)
Wait, wait wait: Do you see her? What a woman.

SERGEANT
She could seed a new cavalry regiment with those hips.

DRUM MAJOR
Or breed a litter of Drum Majors.

SERGEANT
And the way she holds her head! Surprised the weight of the world doesn't drag down that black hair. And those eyes!

DRUM MAJOR
Like looking into the void and coming back nourished. Quick, we must go after her!

> *The DRUM MAJOR runs into the theatre, followed by the Sergeant. The BARKER ushers the rest of the crowd in.*

II.

> *In the Carnival Tent.*
>
> *The BARKER grabs ANDRES from the crowd, slaps a donkey mask and tail onto him and drags him center stage, transforming him into a trained carnival DONKEY.*
>
> *The cast sits among the audience as the BARKER takes center stage and commences the show.*

MARIE

(to the CHILD)
Look at those lights!

WOYZECK
Yes, Marie! Like demon cats with fire eyes! What an evening, huh?

BARKER
(quietly, intensely to the DONKEY)
Show your talents! Show that animal reasoning! Put human society to shame!

> *The BARKER blows his horn in a few staccato toots to get the crowd's attention.*

BARKER
Citizens! Comrades! Look here. The animal you see in front of you - with four hooves and a tail - is a member of our most prestigious philosophical societies and a professor at coastal universities where he teaches the students riding and fighting. Now, let him help us think about thinking. How can you begin to think about thinking when you can't be sure you're even thinking in the first place? Hmm? Is there in an ass in this learned gathering?

> *The DONKEY brays, nods its head, and points at WOYZECK. The BARKER beckons WOYZECK to the stage, with the crowd's support. WOYZECK reluctantly decides to be a good sport. The BARKER takes the donkey mask off of Andres and places it on WOYZECK. They position WOYZECK as the 'head' of the donkey and ANDRES as the 'rear.'*

BARKER
Watch this humble jackass show you how to think about the thoughts you're thinking. It's called…'horse sense'! This is not a dumb animal, no sir. This is a *person* - as good as any human being. A brutish man and yet still - always an animal. A beast. A monster.

> *With a bit of flourish, the DONKEY takes a loud, vulgar 'shit' on the floor, aggressively spraying shaving cream from a contraption within its tail until it piles up beneath its ass. This shaving cream remains on the stage until it is used in a later scene.*

BARKER
That's it! That's it! Lay waste to civilization! You see, the animal is still an animal - human or not. Still in a state of pure, unidealized nature - with no concern for culture or manners. We can all take a lesson from the animal! Even the doctor agrees, it's dangerous to hold it in. Man be natural, they say.
BARKER (cont'd)
You are created of cosmic dust, of sand, of shit! Nothing but the past's garbage. Do you want to be more than the droppings of the past? Look! Look! The reasoning! The logic! Watch this creature count even though it doesn't have fingers!

> *The BARKER holds up four fingers to the DONKEY; like a well-trained carnival animal, WOYZECK stomps four times. The crowd cheers - at the behest of the BARKER. The BARKER pulls a carrot from his pocket and force feeds it to WOYZECK.*

BARKER
See! Look at the way it thinks about thoughts! A shame, really. It can't just express itself and make you understand. But there's humanity in there - it's like a person metamorphosized. Come now, tell the audience what time it is. Will anyone lend us a watch?

DRUM MAJOR
A watch? Here you are, sir!

> *The DRUM MAJOR reveals a pocket watch like a peacock showing off its feathers. MARIE, titillated by the display, climbs toward the front of the audience, leaving her CHILD. MARIE climbs past the DRUM MAJOR and SERGEANT who lasciviously assist her pursuit of a better vantage point.*

DRUM MAJOR
What a woman!

SCENE TRANSITION I

> *Carnival music blares, and the actors that were among the audience rush the stage. Amidst the chaos, WOYZECK lunges for MARIE. She, too, reaches*

for WOYZECK, but before they can meet, the DRUM MAJOR and the SERGEANT scoop up MARIE and carry her away from WOYZECK.

The crowd of actors surges in WOYZECK's direction; he gets swept up in them and dragged off stage - in the opposite direction of MARIE.

The DOCTOR scurries in through the crowd as it drags WOYZECK off and heads directly for the opposite end of the stage in a rush. The CAPTAIN hurries in after the DOCTOR, trying to catch up to them.

III.

On the Street.

The CAPTAIN runs down the middle of the street after the DOCTOR, panting. The CAPTAIN stops to catch their breath and catches sight of the DOCTOR, as well.

CAPTAIN
Doctor! Doctor! Hey, Herr Doctor!

The DOCTOR hears the CAPTAIN but quickens their pace.

CAPTAIN
Don't run away from me! Stop scuttling about like that; the click-clack of your walking stick will drive me mad - like roaches in my skull. What are you racing toward? Death? You know, a decent man is never in a hurry. A decent man with a clear conscience has no need to rush, a decent man…

The CAPTAIN sprints forward and grabs onto the DOCTOR's coat.

CAPTAIN
Doctor, please. Let me save a human life.

DOCTOR
I'm in a hurry, Captain. I'm in a hurry.

CAPTAIN
Doctor, please! I'm so miserable. I can't stop having these fantasies. If I see my coat hanging on the rack, why I just burst into tears. The thought of me, hanging!

The CAPTAIN erupts.

DOCTOR
Hmmm. Yes, well, you're bloated, fat, protuberant veins, yellowing eyes. Apoplectic constitution indeed. Why, yes, Captain, you're on your way to *apoplexia cerebri*. Half of you could get paralyzed, just down one side, if you're lucky or, if we're lucky, your brain will be the only victim and your body will simply vegetate away until you rot like a bag of old meat. This is your prognosis for the next few weeks. You'll be a most interesting case, yes, most interesting indeed. God willing your tongue will be the only thing paralyzed. Then what immortal experiments we will make!

CAPTAIN
(laughing it off)
Doctor! Don't you scare me. People can die of pure fright, of pure fright... Come to think of it, I can already see my funeral. State officials solemnly gathered, mourning efficiently. Sweet singers with lemons in their hands. They'll say I was a decent man - a decent -

While the CAPTAIN loses themself in the fantasy of their funeral, WOYZECK enters the street and tries to furtively pass the CAPTAIN and DOCTOR.

CAPTAIN
Woyzeck! Hey boy! Why are you in such a hurry? Stop with us for a moment, Woyzeck.

WOYZECK approaches the CAPTAIN and stands at attention.

CAPTAIN
My gosh, you run through this world like an open razor! Surprised passersby don't cut themselves on you. You rush about like you've got a regiment of

poorly groomed castrates, eagerly awaiting the touch of your razor. Like you'd be hanged for missing a single hair on an otherwise perfectly shorn scrotum... But, ah! About long beards... What was I saying? Long beards? Woyzeck?

DOCTOR
Wearing a long beard is a habit, as Plinius tells us, that must be forced out of soldiers.

CAPTAIN
Ah, yes! What about those long beards... Woyzeck, have you found any beard hairs in your soup lately? You know what I mean. A human hair from the beard of a private, a sergeant, or a drum major? Well? Woyzeck! No, of course not. He's got an honest wife. Such things could never happen to him.

WOYZECK
Yes, sir! What is it you mean to say to me, sir?

CAPTAIN
If you could look at your own face! Ha! Maybe not so much in your soup. Maybe if you slink around the right corner, you'd find several beard hairs nestled on a pair of lips! Ah, I have also known love, Woyzeck. The man's as white as a sheet.

WOYZECK
Captain, I'm a poor devil. I have nothing in this world, other than my family. Captain, if you're joking with me...

CAPTAIN
Me? Joke? With you? You've got to be joking.

DOCTOR
Your pulse, Woyzeck, your pulse - short, violent, erratic.

WOYZECK
Captain, the Earth is getting hotter every day. It's hotter than hell. But I'm cold - ice cold. Hell's cold too, I bet. Unbelievable! Bitch! The bitch!

CAPTAIN
Do you want a couple of bullets to land in your head? Quit stabbing me with your eyes! I'm only telling you for your own good. Because I like you, Woyzeck. You're a decent man, a decent man.

DOCTOR
(documenting WOYZECK's disposition)
Face muscles now rigid, clenched except for the occasional twitch. Behavior is constrained but excitable. Tense.
WOYZECK
I must be going.

> *WOYZECK turns around and travels back in the direction from which he came, mumbling to himself.*

WOYZECK
It is possible. The bitch! Yes, it's very possible. Anything's possible.

> *WOYZECK turns back and addresses the CAPTAIN.*

WOYZECK
Nice weather today, isn't it, Captain? It's amazing how a beautiful gray sky just makes you want to hammer in a nail so you can hang yourself - all because of the difference between a 'yes' and a 'no.' Can we blame the 'no' for the 'yes' or the 'yes' for the 'no'? I must think about that!

> *WOYZECK leaves first with long slow steps, then with quick short steps.*

DOCTOR
(rushing out after WOYZECK)
What a specimen! Hey, Woyzeck! Let us inspect you! You'll get a raise!

CAPTAIN
That fellow dizzies me. How fast the ogre runs - groping at shadows like a spider - and the little one just runs too. What a storm! Chasing each other like thunder and lightning. Haha! How grotesque! How perfect! Wait for me, Doctor! What about my melancholia?

The CAPTAIN chases after WOYZECK and the DOCTOR.

SCENE TRANSITION II

Klezmer music carries the CAPTAIN out.

Like a changing of the guard, MARIE enters, followed by MARGARET, then the CHILD leading MOTHER by the hand. MARIE settles in and stares out the window of her apartment, out onto the street as MOTHER braids the CHILD's hair.

In the distance, the growing music of the DRUM MAJOR's small parade can be heard as it approaches.

IV.

In MARIE's room. And on the Street.

MARIE holds her CHILD in her lap as she and MARGARET watch for the DRUM MAJOR outside the window.

MARIE
(to the CHILD)
Bum-ba-dada-dum, ba-dada-dum, ba-dada-ba-dada-ba-dada-dum! What's that? Guess who's coming!

The DRUM MAJOR and his small parade walk down the street outside MARIE's window with ostentatious fanfare. The DRUM MAJOR wildly swings a baton, showing off for MARIE.

MARGARET
What a man! Like a tree.

MARIE
He stands on his feet like a bear.

MARGRET
With a lion's beard.

> *The DRUM MAJOR stops his parade below MARIE's window, performs a short routine for her., and then leads the parade out. WOYZECK enters the street as the parade exits, crossing paths with the DRUM MAJOR, which results in a bit of a standoff.*

MARGARET
Oh, giving him the eye, eh? That's not like you, my dear.
MARIE
You're one to talk. Your eyes have been all over everyone, even Grandma wouldn't take them if you offered. And hers haven't worked in years.

MARGARET
Really? You? Well if you aren't the holy virgin yourself! I'm no honest woman, but everyone knows you can stare right through a military uniform.

MARIE
You bitch!

> *MARIE grabs her CHILD's toy and throws it at MARGARET. MARGARET flees. Frightened by the outburst, the CHILD runs to MOTHER. MARIE brings the CHILD to her and forcibly comforts them.*

MARIE
Shhh, shhh, come now, my child. People will always talk. You might be the child of a poor whore, but you're still my pride and joy. Just look at this angel-face. There, there...

> *MARIE rocks the child and sings a lullaby.*

MARIE
(singing)
How can we tame those wild eyes?
What will we do if the whole world dies?

*There's nothing to do but sit here and sing
and rockabye, rockabye, poor little thing.
There's nothing to be and nothing to do…*

> *As she's singing, WOYZECK enters, shrouded in shadows. He watches.
> Moved by her song, WOYZECK emits a soft whimper that startles MARIE.*

MARIE
Is someone there? Hello?

> *MARIE leaves the CHILD with MOTHER and approaches.*

MARIE
Franz, is that you? What are you doing out there? Come in.

WOYZECK
I can't. Got to go.

MARIE
Been chopping wood for the Captain?
WOYZECK
Yes, Marie.

> *WOYZECK steps into the light.*

MARIE
Franz? What's wrong? You look wild.

WOYZECK
Things, Marie. Things have been happening again. More things. It's been getting hotter. Isn't it written - 'and there was a great smoke emanating from the land, as if from an oven, as if the land itself was a torch…'

MARIE
Franz!

WOYZECK

It followed me until I got to town. Something. I could feel its heat. Something we don't understand, something that will drive us mad.

MARIE
Franz!

WOYZECK
I've got to go. At the fair tonight, then, yes? I've put aside a bit for us.

WOYZECK leaves in a frenzy.

MARIE
What a man. He's losing it! He didn't so much as look at his child. Thinking will drive him mad. He needs more work.

MARIE notices the CHILD, cowering.

MARIE
Why are you so quiet, child? No need to be frightened. I know, it's so dark you could think you were blind. We're all like you now, Mother. Usually the moon shines through the window. I can't stand it! I'm shaking, too!

SCENE TRANSITION III

MARIE grabs the CHILD and carries them out, close to her breast. MOTHER blindly ambles after them.

ANDRES whistles as he walks in with WOYZECK, who engages in wild perfunctory stealth maneuvers to ensure no one is following them. They both carry axes. They find a prime spot and settle in to split firewood for their regiment.

V.

In a Field on the outskirts of town.

ANDRES and WOYZECK are splitting wood. ANDRES whistles to himself.

WOYZECK
This place is cursed, Andres. Yes, it is. Can't you feel the heat? See that patch of light over there - where the mushrooms grow? That's where you can see the old head roll by in the evenings. Someone picked the head up once. He thought it was a hedgehog. But no hedgehogs here. Just that cursed head, rolling by with no body in sight. Three days and three nights later, he was sealed in his coffin. It was the freemasons, I'm telling you. I'm sure of it. The freemasons! Shhh!

ANDRES
(singing to himself)
Too many bunnies,
filling up their tummies
eating all the grass
till green drips out their -

WOYZECK
Shhh! Do you hear it, Andres? Something's moving.

ANDRES
(continuing to sing to himself)
Digging in the dirt
till they tear up the earth.
And -

WOYZECK
Shhhh! It's here, Andres! Something's behind me. Or beneath me!

WOYZECK stomps on the ground. He listens. He stomps and listens again.

WOYZECK
You see? It's hollow. Completely hollow under here. The freemasons!

ANDRES
I'm scared, Franz.

WOYZECK
Shhh! Strange. It's so quiet you want to hold your breath. Andres?

ANDRES
What?

WOYZECK
Say something.

>   *Silence.*

WOYZECK
Wow, Andres, it's so bright! Can you see the town glowing in the distance? Fire's shooting across the sky. And look, down here - a sound like trumpets! They want to seduce me! Quick, don't look behind you!

>   *WOYZECK grabs ANDRES and drags him into the bushes. They hide, silent. A pause.*

ANDRES
Franz, you still hear it?

WOYZECK
It's silent, completely silent. Like everything is dead.

>   *Suddenly, military drums resound in the distance.*

ANDRES
Wait - what was that? Oh, the drums. We'd better head back to town.

SCENE TRANSITION IV

>   *ANDRES runs out.*

WOYZECK runs after him, but he's intercepted by the DRUM MAJOR's parade, followed by the DOCTOR.

The DRUM MAJOR and his cronies grab a hold of WOYZECK. They lift him above their heads and carry him to the center of the space, quickly stripping him naked in the process - almost like a magic trick. They set WOYZECK on his feet in the center of the space and march off as the DOCTOR wheels in a small laboratory cart loaded with primitive and intimidating scientific instruments.

VI.

In the DOCTOR's Laboratory.

WOYZECK stands nude, stationary with his arms extended, as though strapped to an invisible examination table. The DOCTOR rummages through medical equipment and interrogates WOYZECK.

DOCTOR
What's this about, Woyzeck? What's this! A man of his word?

WOYZECK
What is it, Doctor?

DOCTOR
I saw you, Woyzeck, I saw you. You pissed in the street! You pissed against the wall - like a dog! And three dollars a day - plus food. A waste. What a waste. Woyzeck, this is bad. The world is turning bad, very bad!

WOYZECK
But Doctor, when Nature calls, I -

DOCTOR
Nature? When nature calls... Nature! Haven't I proven that the urethra is subject to man's will? Nature! Man is free, Woyzeck. Man's very Nature is to

be free of anything like Nature! Couldn't hold his piss! Are you eating your peas, Woyzeck? Nothing but peas for you, remember that! You're very important to our studies, Woyzeck, and peas are the key! We're re-making science here, blowing the past to pieces! Uric acid, point two. Ammonia hypochlorite, yes. Chloride, yes. Potassium, yes. Creatine... Woyzeck, don't you need to let out some more piss? Go ahead. Try.

> *The DOCTOR holds a vessel below WOYZECK's penis. He tries to piss several times but fails to produce anything.*

WOYZECK
I can't, Doctor.

DOCTOR
But you could piss against a wall! I have our contract in my hand! That's your signature, is it not? I saw it. I saw it with my own eyes. I had just stuck my head
DOCTOR (cont'd)
out the window for my afternoon observations on staring at the sun and there you - No, Woyzeck, I'm *not* getting angry. I'm not *angry*. Anger is unhealthy. It's unscientific. I am calm. I'm quite calm. My pulse is at its usual sixty-two, and I can assert with the utmost calm... CAN'T WE HAVE A HUMAN BEING AS A SUBJECT AND NOT THIS ANIMAL! A human being, a human being... Now, were you a paramecium! But really, Woyzeck, you really shouldn't have pissed against the wall.

WOYZECK
Well, Doctor, the thing is - I - well, sometimes, one is... of such structure, of a system. But with Nature... I am - kind of a... there is a character that...

DOCTOR
You're philosophizing again.

WOYZECK
Doctor, have you ever witnessed a duality? A true double nature? Everyday, when the sun is highest in the sky, it's like the world is burning, like it's on fire. That's when the voice speaks to me.

DOCTOR
You're an aberration, Woyzeck! A beautiful aberration!

WOYZECK
(shaking his head 'no')
It's in the mushrooms, Doctor. That's where. Have you noticed the patterns they make on the ground? They're trying to tell us something, if only we could understand them.

DOCTOR
You are the finest aberration, Woyzeck! Of the second category, quite severe. You deserve a raise, Woyzeck. Second category: single obsession but otherwise sound. Well then. How are things? Everything good? Shaving the Captain?

WOYZECK
Yes, Doctor.
DOCTOR
Eating your peas?

WOYZECK
Yes, all of them, Doctor. I give my wife the money for -

DOCTOR
Maintaining your civic duties?

WOYZECK
Yes, sir.

DOCTOR
You're a good egg, Woyzeck. And a great case. Yes, a great case. You're on track for a raise one day. Just keep it up. Shall we feel your pulse? That's it. Yes.

SCENE TRANSITION V

The DOCTOR pushes his medical cart out as WOYZECK, still nude, marches off stage in the opposite direction.

MARIE wanders in wearing earrings that shine like stars and staring into a hand mirror. The CHILD follows, with MOTHER.

VII.

In MARIE's apartment.

The CHILD tugs at MARIE's dress. MOTHER sleeps in a chair.

MARIE
(brushing the CHILD off)
He got his orders and he had to go! What else could he do?

MARIE resumes consuming her reflection.

MARIE
Oh, how they sparkle! What kind did he say they are? Shhh, my child, sleep! Close those eyes hard. Tighter still. Or else the sand man will come and steal you.

MARIE sings the CHILD a haunting lullaby.

MARIE
(singing)
Your eyes you must close very tight
when you sleep or else at night
the refugee will steal your hand
and lead you off to no man's land

The CHILD sleeps. MARIE stares at her reflection.

MARIE
They're definitely real. How they'll shine when we dance! All I have in this world is this room and this broken mirror! Yet my lips are as red as any lady of leisure with her mirrors, floor to ceiling, fine pastries, and a real gentleman to kiss her hand. Who am I kidding? I'm just a poor woman.

MARIE's talking stirs the CHILD.

MARIE
Settle down, child. Make yourself sleep. In sleep, you'll have no worries. Keep those eyes shut! If the sandman sees your eyes, they'll be his soon enough!

MARIE dances around, humming waltz music to herself. WOYZECK enters behind her and tries to dance with her. Startled, MARIE jumps away and covers her ears.

WOYZECK
What's that there, Marie?

MARIE
What?

WOYZECK
It's still shining. I can see it.

MARIE
It's nothing. An earring. I found it.

WOYZECK
How strange, Marie. I've never been lucky enough to find anything, but you've found two of the same.

MARIE
I have good luck.

WOYZECK

I'm happy for you, Marie. Look, how the child sleeps. It's not good for a child, sleeping like that. Too hot. The little lad's covered in sweat! Ah, there's nothing but work, work in the sun for people like us. We must still sweat in our sleep, us poor folk. Here. I've more money, Marie. All my pay and some extra from the Captain.

MARIE
You're a saint, Franz.

WOYZECK
I must go. Tonight, Marie.

> *WOYZECK leaves. After a beat:*

MARIE
Oh, I'm a naughty girl, aren't I? I could just stab myself! The world is hell, anyway. We're all going to hell.

SCENE TRANSITION VI

> *ANDRES marches in as WOYZECK tries to exit. MARIE runs off, away from ANDRES. The CHILD wakes MOTHER, and they leave together, following MARIE.*
> *ANDRES hands WOYZECK a rifle and redirects him. He begrudgingly marches back on stage and into the barracks.*

VIII.

> *In the Barracks.*
>
> *ANDRES and WOYZECK clean their rifles.*

ANDRES
(singing)
The lady would have a maid
If such plans the world had laid.

Instead she has to toil away,
Exhaustion haunting every day -

WOYZECK
Andres.

ANDRES
Yes?

WOYZECK
Nice weather.

ANDRES
Summer weather. There's music in town, and the women are coming. Everybody's sweating. I like it.

WOYZECK
Dancing! They're dancing, Andres.

ANDRES
Yes, at the Inn.

WOYZECK
Dancing, dancing!

ANDRES
Yeah, so what?
Every day she sits in her window
To watch the regiments pass below
Longing for a life not hers -

WOYZECK
Andres! I can't stay still!

ANDRES
Quiet, you idiot!

WOYZECK
My head is spinning, Andres. Spinning. It's hot. I have to go. Dancing, dancing! Will her hands be hot? Will they? Andres!

ANDRES
What?

WOYZECK
I have to go quickly. I need to see.

ANDRES
You're a fool. All this for her?

WOYZECK
I have to go! It's too hot in here!

SCENE TRANSITION VII

ANDRES kisses WOYZECK on the cheek and leaves.

The CAPTAIN enters, along with a small chorus of SOLDIERS. In militaristic fashion, the CAPTAIN removes their coat and boots and hands them to the SOLDIERS. The SOLDIERS sit, hanging on every word from the CAPTAIN while mending their clothes and shining their boots.

WOYZECK puts on a barber's apron and scoops up the pile of shaving cream the HORSE previously shat onto the ground. The CAPTAIN sits in a spinning barber's chair and beckons WOYZECK.

IX.

In the Captain's office.

WOYZECK lathers the CAPTAIN and shaves them.

CAPTAIN
Slower, Woyzeck! Slower. Take your god given time. You're making me dizzy! What's a Captain to do with the few minutes you save here, hmm? Just think about it. You've got thirty years of life left, Woyzeck! Thirty years, at least! That's - 360 months! And…days, hours. Minutes! How can a man like you use that time? Slow down. Take your time, Woyzeck.

WOYZECK
Yes, Captain.

CAPTAIN
Oh, Woyzeck. I worry about the world when I think about time. Eternity is far too long a thing to consider. It pains my soul to think about it. Stay busy, Woyzeck, and you'll escape eternity. That's forever, you know? Forever! And then again, to something else, to someone else, it's not eternity but a passing moment. The blink of an eye, Woyzeck. My blood runs cold when I remember the world spins all the way around every day! Ah! It's such a waste of time. And how will it all end? I only have to look at a top spinning and I'm full of dread.

WOYZECK
Yes, Captain.

CAPTAIN
Woyzeck, you look so…haunted. A decent man wouldn't. A decent man with a clear conscience… Well? Say something, Woyzeck! Anything. What kind of weather is it today?

WOYZECK
Unpleasant, sir. Windy.

CAPTAIN
I can feel it passing through me! It's such a rush. The wind makes me giddy like a mouse. What do you think, Woyzeck? That's wind's blowing from the…northern south?

WOYZECK

Yes, Captain.

CAPTAIN
Haha! Northern south!

The SOLDIERS dutifully laugh at the CAPTAIN's gag.

CAPTAIN
Oh, lord, Woyzeck, you're so horribly stupid. You're a decent man, but you have no morals. Morality is…when a person is moral, you understand? Moral's a good word. The church hasn't blessed your marriage or your child. As our righteous Reverend Preacher said, no church blessing. I didn't say that.

WOYZECK
Captain, sir, the Lord won't look down on the little varmint because no one said "Amen" before he was made. The Lord himself said, "Suffer the little children that come unto me."

CAPTAIN
What was that? Very weird answer, Woyzeck. He makes me quite confused with his answers. And I don't mean "He"; I mean you.

WOYZECK
Captain, it's - we poor folk, you see, it's money. When you haven't any money, morals won't do. You can't raise a child on morals alone. We have needs. Man is flesh and blood like the animals. The poor are never blessed, in this world or the next. I'm sure if we get to heaven, we'll have to help keep the place clean.

CAPTAIN
But Woyzeck, you have no virtue! You are simply not a virtuous man. Flesh and blood? Pssst. Look, when it's raining and the world's stuffed me with misery, I peer out the window and watch the maiden's tripping down cobblestones - damnit Woyzeck - I feel love in my loins. I know that I too am blood and flesh. But it's - virtue! Virtue, Woyzeck, virtue! Without virtue, how does a man know how best to spend his time? So, I say to myself, "You are a virtuous man. A decent man, a decent man!"

WOYZECK
Yes, Captain, sir. Virtue. Lucky for me, I don't have that problem. Us ordinary people can't have virtue. We follow our natures. But, if like you, I was an aristocrat. If I had a hat or a watch or a cane with a wool overcoat and could speak several languages, then maybe I could be virtuous. I'd like to be virtuous, but I'm a poor man.

CAPTAIN
This is good, Woyzeck, very good. You are a decent man. But you think too much. It weighs you down. You look haunted. I feel a wave of misery coming on, thanks to you. Go now. I must be alone.

WOYZECK hesitantly removes his apron, then starts to run out.

CAPTAIN
But don't run like that.

The CAPTAIN gestures and the SOLDIERS bring their coat and boots and help the CAPTAIN dress.

CAPTAIN
Slowly, nice and slowly down the road. Yes, just like that. Never be in a rush. There's too much time to fill as it is.

SCENE TRANSITION XVIII

WOYZECK continues leaving slowly, as the CAPTAIN leads the SOLDIERS out in a march.

As WOYZECK moves slowly, the sounds of dancing at the Inn grow louder. SOLDIERS, DRINKERS, and much of the cast cross the stage dancing a fast-paced waltz. MARIE and the DRUM MAJOR dance passionately together.

WOYZECK continues moving unnaturally slow until the CAPTAIN and the SOLDIERS exit. As soon as they do, WOYZECK breaks out into a sprint.

X.

Outside the Inn.

The shadows of dancing patrons and the sound of raucous music flows from the Inn's open windows. Two APPRENTICES exit the Inn, very drunk and still dancing.

APPRENTICE #1
(singing)
This shirt I'm wearing isn't mine!
My soul stinks is of brandywine!

APPRENTICE #2
Friend! Shall I punch a hole right through your face, brother? For friendship? Listen, as one friend to another friend, I'll do it. I'll punch a hole through you! I'm a man too. I can say that! I'll knock the piss outta anyone.

APPRENTICE #1
My life stinks of brandywine. Everything rots. Even money. It's beautiful, isn't it? I could cry enough tears to fill a trough to drown myself. All this misery. I wish both our tears were wine so we could pour them down each other's throats!

WOYZECK runs in, frenzied, scaring the APPRENTICES. He stands by the window and watches MARIE and the DRUM MAJOR dance. They don't see him.

WOYZECK
The two of them! Damn! On and on, and on and on. It all keeps spinning, keeps turning, whirling. Why won't God snuff out the sun? No, no, that's all they need - darkness so they can slather themselves in lust. Woman and man! Woman and beast! Beast and man! Here, in broad daylight. Devil! They'll do

it in the palm of my hand like flies. She's hot. Look at her hot hands. On and on, on and on. Spinning, turning. He's grabbing her body. Like it is at the beginning. Turning, spinning. Spinning, turning. On and on, on and on!

WOYZECK collapses. APPRENTICE #1 gives a speech to his limp body.

APPRENTICE #1
Yes, every once in a while some wretch like you stands waist-deep in the river of time and challenges God by asking "Why does man exist?" "Why does man exist?" But me? I pull that man out of time before he drowns. And I tell him - how would a farmer or a doctor live if man didn't exist? How would a tailor make money if God didn't make men feel shame? And how could a soldier live, if God didn't fill him with the need to be killed? Have no doubts! We can have the good, delicious pleasures of this world, but everything is still vanity. Everything rots. Even money. So… hey, relax, I'm getting to my point! My point is: let's all go piss on the cross to show God what we think of this hell he's made for us!

SCENE TRANSITION IX

The APPRENTICE prepares to pee on WOYZECK. WOYZECK wakes up, and the APPRENTICE pretends like they were doing something else.

Everyone filters out of the Inn, drunk and joyous. The DRUM MAJOR lovingly scoops up MARIE and carries her away from the Inn. He sets her on her feet and she coyly walks in front of him, leading the way to her room as the DRUM MAJOR strips off his clothes till he's in just shoes, socks, and underwear.

WOYZECK watches and follows, unnoticed.

XI.

In Marie's room.

The DRUM MAJOR follows MARIE into her room like a proud predator.

WOYZECK watches, from a distance.

DRUM MAJOR
Marie!

MARIE
Let me watch you walk. Come on. Chest like a buffalo, beard like a lion. I'm the luckiest lady alive.

DRUM MAJOR
Have you seen me on Sundays? When I've got my feathered helmet and my fancy gloves - good lord! Even the prince will say, "What a man!"

MARIE
(flirtatiously mocking)
Does he? Really?

DRUM MAJOR
And you're one magnificent woman! Just imagine the brood of Drum Majors that'll come from these hips.

The DRUM MAJOR pulls MARIE into his embrace.

MARIE
(seriously)
Let me go!

DRUM MAJOR
You animal!

MARIE

(violent, like a caged animal)
Get your hands off me!

DRUM MAJOR
I can see the Devil in your eyes.

MARIE
Who cares? We're all going to hell anyway.

> *MARIE strips off her clothes and presents herself to the DRUM MAJOR.*

SCENE TRANSITION X

> *MARIE jumps on the DRUM MAJOR and they tumble and twirl, spinning their way off stage as MARIE allows herself to be ravaged.*
>
> *WOYZECK tries to follow, but ANDRES enters and pulls him away from MARIE.*

XII.

> *In the Barracks at night.*
>
> *ANDRES and WOYZECK are in the same bed. ANDRES sleeps peacefully. WOYZECK is restless.*

WOYZECK
Andres! Andres! Hey, Andres!

ANDRES
What - what - what is it?

WOYZECK
I can't sleep. I'm spinning, Andres. When I close my eyes, the world goes round and round. I hear music. On and on and on and on. And the walls, they speak. You don't hear anything?

ANDRES
Just let her dance. What's it to you? Now let me sleep. May God keep us. Amen.

WOYZECK
They're saying "Stab, stab, stab!" I hear it between my eyes - like a knife in my brain.

ANDRES
You have a fever. Let me get you brandy and a painkiller. That'll help.

WOYZECK
No, I'm quite well.

ANDRES
Then sleep, you madman.

> *ANDRES turns away from WOYZECK and falls back asleep.*

WOYZECK
On and on. On and on and on and on.

SCENE TRANSITION XI

> *ANDRES leaves.*
>
> *WOYZECK paces manically around the stage. MARIE and the CHILD enter, and WOYZECK circles them like a shark as they make their way towards MARIE's room.*

XIII.

In MARIE's room.

The CHILD sleeps. MARIE stands between WOYZECK and the CHILD. WOYZECK paces, stammering and shaking his head.

WOYZECK
Hmm. Well. I don't see anything. Nothing. It should be real. I should see it. You should be able to hold it.

MARIE
What is it? Franz? You're raving.

WOYZECK
A sin, Marie! I can smell it! A big hot rotten sin. It stinks so much the angels in heaven will soon vomit on our heads. Look, Marie. Your mouth is red. No sores? No sin is as tempting as you Marie. How can the Lord tempt us with a mortal sin so beautiful.

MARIE
Franz, you're out of your mind.

WOYZECK
Demon! He stood here, huh? How, Marie? Like this? Like this? This?

MARIE
The world is old, Franz. Many different people have stood in the same place.

WOYZECK
I saw him.

MARIE
Well, you have two eyes. So you should see plenty if the sun's shining and they haven't fallen out yet.

WOYZECK
Bitch!

MARIE
Don't touch me, Franz. I'd rather a knife in my gut than your flesh on mine. You know nothing, Franz. Even my father learned not to touch me, not since I looked him in the eyes.

WOYZECK
No, Marie, no. There's something wrong with you. You're a hot abyss. The world is spinning so fast I get dizzy when I look down. Maybe. Maybe you're innocent. You look like Innocence. But, I say to you: Innocence, you're rotten on the inside. It's gotten too hot. Do you know I know? Do I know? Does anyone?

SCENE TRANSITION XII

MARIE rushes out, bringing the CHILD with her.

WOYZECK puts his ear to the ground and listens. The CAPTAIN, the DRUM MAJOR, and the SERGEANT enter - gossiping like old pals. They look at WOYZECK and laugh.

ANDRES follows them, timidly, carrying a basket of boots.

XIV.

In the Barracks.

ANDRES polishes boots, listening for a conversation in the adjoining room. WOYZECK slinks in.

WOYZECK
Have you heard anything?

ANDRES

He's still in there. With some friends.

WOYZECK
He must have said something.

ANDRES
And you'd know? What do you think he said? "He laughed. Said she was so hot. Great body, red mouth, tasted like figs from tip to tail!"

WOYZECK
Huh. So that's what he said, is it? What did I dream the other night? Something about a knife? Some people have very dumb dreams.

>*WOYZECK starts to leave.*

ANDRES
Where do you think you're going, Franz?

WOYZECK
To fetch provisions for my officer. Wine, women, sundries. Andres - she was the only girl.

ANDRES
What?

WOYZECK
Nothing.

SCENE TRANSITION XIII

>*WOYZECK and ANDRES part ways, leaving in opposite directions.*
>
>*The DRUM MAJOR, the SERGEANT, SOLDIERS, the two APPRENTICES, MOTHER, and a group of DRINKERS enter, already celebrating the evening. They make their way across the stage, transforming it from the Barracks to the Inn along the way.*

XV.

In the Inn.

The DRUM MAJOR, the two APPRENTICES, a chorus of SOLDIERS, and a group of DRINKERS dance about the Inn. MOTHER, who is also the barmaid, tends bar.

DRUM MAJOR
I'm a man! A man I said! Who wants some, huh? Unless you're jesus christ or the devil himself - and pissed too - you better stay away from me. I'll punch your nose till it falls out your ass. A man has to drink - a man -

WOYZECK enters, heading for MOTHER and trying to skirt the action.

DRUM MAJOR
(to WOYZEKCK)
Hey! You! Drink! Schnapps! I wish the whole world were schnapps!

WOYZECK whistles.

DRUM MAJOR
You! Shall I tear your innards out your ass and tie them around your throat?

WOYZECK rips off his jacket and puts his fists up. The DRUM MAJOR invites him to punch first, and WOYZECK punches the DRUM MAJOR square on the jaw. The DRUM MAJOR barely flinches. WOYZECK tries to tackle the DRUM MAJOR, but the DRUM MAJOR knocks him to the ground. He climbs on top of WOYZECK and pummels. It continues - a brutal, one-sided fight. WOYZECK tries to get up several times. He lands a few hits, but they don't have a chance of impacting the outcome. WOYZECK loses horribly - bruised and bloodied, his clothes torn.

As the fight escalates, the crowd falls to their haunches and barks like a pack of rabid dogs. Finally, THE DRUM MAJOR picks WOYZECK up by his throat and slams him into the ground, ending the fight. The moment

WOYZECK hits the ground, the crowd stops barking and starts laughing, slowly returning to their normal way of being.

DRUM MAJOR
I won't leave you enough breath for an old lady's fart!

WOYZECK remains on the ground, winded and injured. THE DRUM MAJOR dumps his drink on WOYZECK.

DRUM MAJOR
Now you can whistle till you're blue in the face.

The DRUM MAJOR rallies the crowd and leads them out of the Inn in an improvised victory parade

DRUM MAJOR
(singing)
Brandywine, it is my life!
Brandywine, it gives you courage!

SCENE TRANSITION XIV

The DRUM MAJOR continues his drunken parade, leading the crowd in song and dance until they leave the stage.

WOYZECK remains on the ground as the Inn transforms into a Field on the outskirts of town. He stands up uneasily, as if his head his spinning, like he has vertigo.

XVI.

In a Field.

WOYZECK
On and on, on and on. Squeak and squeal go the fiddles and the pipes. On and on, on and on. Stop! Stop the music! Who's talking down there?

WOYZECK puts his ear to the ground and listens to the voices coming up through the Earth.

WOYZECK
What? What's that you say? Louder! Louder! Stab her? Stab her dead. Shall I? Must I? Do I hear it up there too? Is the wind saying it? I can hear it echoing on the leaves - on and on, on and on. Stab her dead! Dead!

SCENE TRANSITION XV

The DOCTOR enters, followed by a group of MEDICAL STUDENTS.

WOYZECK gets up and tries to avoid them, but the DOCTOR grabs him by the ear and drags him into the laboratory.

XVII.

In the Doctor's lab.

The DOCTOR lectures from a pedestal as MEDICAL STUDENTS take notes. WOYZECK stands at attention, observing the class.

DOCTOR
Gentlemen, I often find myself on the roof admiring the world - like David when he saw Bathsheba. Except I don't see anything except the girls' knickers hanging on the line in the school yard.

The MEDICAL STUDENTS dutifully chuckle.

DOCTOR
Gentlemen, we are now examining the subject's relation to the object. Let us take a creature in which we see the highest manifestation of divinity and examine its relationship to space, the earth, the cosmos. For example, gentlemen, if I were to throw this cat high in the air, how will this creature, in accordance with its nature, maintain its center of gravity?

The DOCTOR throws the cat high in the air, like a fly ball. Its trajectory points directly to WOYZECK's head.

DOCTOR
Hello there, Woyzeck. Woyzeck!

WOYZECK catches the cat.

WOYZECK
It bit me, Doctor!

DOCTOR
(to the STUDENTS)
He holds the beast as if it were his own flesh and blood.

WOYZECK
(attempting to tenderly hold the aggravated cat)
I can't stop shaking, Doctor.

DOCTOR
Ah, ah, wonderful, Woyzeck.

The DOCTOR takes the cat and holds it up to the STUDENTS.

DOCTOR
What we have here, gentlemen, is a new species of rabbit-louse, a marvelous, parasitic species…

The DOCTOR takes out a magnifying glass to examine the cat. The cat screeches and claws at the DOCTOR. The DOCTOR throws the cat over their shoulder.

DOCTOR
Gentlemen, animals have no scientific instincts. But here is something else to observe!

The DOCTOR grabs WOYZECK and displays him for the STUDENTS.

DOCTOR
See this man here? For three months he's eaten nothing but peas! Can you see the effects? Just feel him. What an irregular pulse. And look at the eyes!

WOYZECK
It's all gone black, Doctor.

DOCTOR
Courage, Woyzeck. Just a few more days and then it'll all be over. Come. Feel him, Gentlemen.

>*The STUDENTS palpate WOYZECK - his neck, his chest, his groin. They feel his pulse, the tautness of skin. They shine penlights in his eyes.*

DOCTOR
Ah, yes, Woyzeck, wiggle your ears for the gentlemen. I wanted to show you all this - these two small muscles he uses, together. Really spectacular - like a lesser beast. Wiggle away, Woyzeck.

WOYZECK
But Doctor…

DOCTOR
Do I have to wiggle your ears for you? You wretch! You want to follow the cat's example, eh?

>*WOYZECK wiggles his ears.*

DOCTOR
That's it. Now, gentlemen, you see, he's wiggling his ears, a sign of his transformation into a donkey. This, in fact, is a consequence of being brought up by a female and using the mother tongue. Tell us, Woyzeck, how many strands of hair has your mother, out of pure fondness, plucked for mementos? It is getting quite thin on top these past few days. Yes, gentlemen, the secret is peas.

SCENE TRANSITION XVI

The DOCTOR and the MEDICAL STUDENTS march out.

ANDRES enters, solemnly. WOYZECK grabs his rucksack and meets him.

XVIII.

In the Barracks.

WOYZECK sorts his personal possessions, offering some to ANDRES.

WOYZECK
This jacket isn't standard issue. You might like to have it.

ANDRES
Yes.

WOYZECK
The cross and the ring I found by the pond.

ANDRES
Yes.

WOYZECK
And I have this icon too - two hearts and real gold. It was in my mother's bible. I found it where it says, "Lord, like thy body, red and sore, so let my heart be evermore." My mother can't read any more. She can't feel anything anymore - only when the sun shines on her. It won't matter.

ANDRES
Yes.

WOYZECK
(reading from his enlistment papers)

Friedrich Johann Franz Woyzeck, rifleman, fourth company, second battalion, second regiment, born on the Feast of the Annunciation, 20th July. Today I am 30 years, seven months and twelve days old.

ANDRES
Franz, you'll end up in the looney bin. You need some schnapps with gunpowder in it. That'll kill your fever.

WOYZECK
Sure, Andres. And when the carpenter nails two boards together, no one knows whose head will be laid to rest on them.

SCENE TRANSITION XVII

ANDRES leaves, as if to a dirge, carrying WOYZECK's rucksack.

MARIE enters, absorbed in her bible. The CHILD leads MOTHER by the hand, playing a game along the way.

WOYZECK remains where he is and watches the next scene.

XIX.

In MARIE's room.

MARIE desperately pages through her bible while MOTHER entertains the CHILD.

MOTHER
The sausage said, "This one's got the gold crown. He's the lord king. Tomorrow I'll get the queen her child back." "Come now, Sausage," said the Black Pudding.

MARIE

(reading)
'Nor was guile found in his mouth…' Lord, please don't look at me.

She turns more pages.

MARIE
(reading)
'And they brought to him a woman taken in adultery and set her in the midst… and Jesus said unto her, "Neither do I condemn thee. Go and sin no more."' My god, my god, I can't! Oh lord, just forgive me enough so I can pray.

The CHILD tries to get MARIE to play with them.

MARIE
It breaks my heart to look at you, Child. A knife in my heart. Stop basking in the sun and help me with this Child.

MOTHER takes CHILD.

MARIE
Franz hasn't been here. Not today, not yesterday. Oh, it is getting too hot in here. Everything is dead. Savior, savior! If only someone like me could anoint your feet!

WOYZECK enters the room.

WOYZECK
Marie.

MARIE
What is it?

WOYZECK
We're going now, Marie. It's time.

MARIE
Where?

WOYZECK
Why should I know?

SCENE TRANSITION XVIII

> *WOYZECK takes MARIE by the hand and takes her on a meandering path out of town.*

XX.

> *By a Pond, on the outskirts of town.*

> *WOYZECK leads MARIE through the reeds.*

MARIE
Is that the town over there? It's looks so dark.

WOYZECK
Come, sit down.

MARIE
I have to get back.

WOYZECK
You don't have to go anywhere.

MARIE
What's gotten into you?

WOYZECK
Do you know how long it's been, Marie?
MARIE
Two years come summer's end.

WOYZECK
Do you know how long it's going to be?

MARIE
I have to go. It's time to make supper.

WOYZECK
Are you cold, Marie? You look cold. And yet it's so hot. You're so hot, Marie. I can feel it coming off you. You're on fire. What hot lips you've got. Hot! So hot they rot. Still, I'd give everything under the sun to kiss them again... Are you cold? It's okay. When you're cold you won't feel cold anymore.

MARIE
What are you saying.

WOYZECK
Nothing.

MARIE
The moon's rising. It's so red.

WOYZECK
Like blood shining on a blade.

MARIE
You're so pale, Franz.

WOYZECK reveals a knife and raises it menacingly.

MARIE
Franz! No, Franz! For God's sake -

MARIE tries to run away. WOYZECK stabs ferociously.

MARIE
Franz! No! Help! Please! Franz! Franz, why are you - Franz!

WOYZECK
There! Take that! And that! What? You can't die? There! Have another! There! Still twitching, still turning, not soon. Not yet. Another! Once more!

He stabs one final time, leaving the knife in MARIE's body.

WOYZECK
Are you dead? Dead! Dead!

As WOYZECK takes a moment to consider the scene, the two APPRENTICES enter, trudging back toward town.

APPRENTICE #1
Stop!

APPRENTICE #2
You hear it too? Quiet. That!

APPRENTICE #1
Oh, what a sound!

APPRENTICE #2
It's the water, sending out its siren song. It's been awhile since someone drowned. Let's go. It's not good to hear this.

WOYZECK whimpers and sobs as he tries to put MARIE back together. The APPRENTICES stop and consider heading in the direction of the sounds.

APPRENTICE #1
There it is again! Sounds like someone dying. We should see.

APPRENTICE #2
It's eerie. So dark and foggy. And the beetle's buzzing like death's knell. Come on, let's go see!

The APPRENTICES decide to investigate the sounds. WOYZECK runs off, bumping into them along the way.

SCENE TRANSITION XIX

MARIE's body remains where it is. SOLDIERS, DANCERS, MOTHER, and the rest of the Inn crowd enter, drinking and chatting.

They step over MARIE's corpse as though it wasn't there.

XXI.

In the Inn.

MOTHER tends bar as DANCERS, DRINKERS, and SOLDIERS enjoy the evening. WOYZECK stampedes into the Inn, in a deliriously good mood, covered with MARIE's blood.

WOYZECK
Yes, dance! Dance everyone. On and on! Keep turning on and on till it gets too hot! Ah the stink of sweat! Life! He'll take you all in the end anyway.

WOYZECK grabs a patron and dances, singing along to the music.

WOYZECK
(singing)
Oh shame my dear wife
What's this you've done?
Bedded down with a soldier
And polished his gun!

WOYZECK removes his clothes as he dances. The CROWD is both shocked and bemused.

WOYZECK

The devil's made it hot in here! Sure he might take one of us, but he let the other one go! Come, Mother. Let me see if you're warm too.

WOYZECK walks to MOTHER and makes her sit down.

WOYZECK
Oh, you're warm too. I wonder why. Doesn't matter. You'll be cold one day soon. Even you. Sing me a song, Mother.

WOYZECK drapes his body across his MOTHER's lap, like the Pieta.

MOTHER
(singing)
A little boy upon a knee
Must never cry or ask of me
For finer things than linen clothes
and women wearing pantyhose.

WOYZECK
No, no clothes. You can't get to Hell with them on.

Trying to quiet WOYZECK, MOTHER puts her hands on his. She feels the blood still on them.

MOTHER
What's on your hand?

MOTHER tastes her fingers.

MOTHER
Blood?!

A CROWD gathers round them. WOYZECK jumps from his MOTHER's lap and gathers his clothes as he heads for the exit. The CROWD moves to block his path, brooding and inching forward - like a preying pod of orcas.

WOYZECK

Blood? Blood?

The CROWD
Blood! Blood!
WOYZECK
I think I cut my hand.

SERGEANT
Then how's there blood on your elbow?

WOYZECK
I wiped it off!

MOTHER
I smell the blood of a woman!

> *In unison, the CROWD chants "Fe Fi Fo Fum" over and over as they slowly close in on WOYZECK.*

WOYZECK
What the Hell do you want? Want to come to Hell too? What's it got to do with you! Out of my way! I'm a soldier! …You think I've killed someone? Am I a murderer? Can a soldier be a murderer? What are you staring at! You're better off staring at yourselves if it's guilt you're looking for. Get out of my way!

> *WOYZECK rushes through the CROWD and leaves.*

SCENE TRANSITION XX

> *WOYZECK runs as if demons are chasing him. The CROWD slowly scatters in all directions.*

> *The APPRENTICES make their way towards MARIE's body, hiding themselves in the brush.*

XXII.

By the Pond, outside of town.

The APPRENTICES search.

APPRENTICE #1
Can you see it?

APPRENTICE #2
What?

APPRENTICE #1
Looks like someone's laying over there.

APPRENTICE #2
Where?

APPRENTICE #1
Over there. Past the ditch by the pond.

APPRENTICE #2
Let's go. We've got to see!

APPRENTICE #1
Shhh! Stay hidden! Sounds like someone's coming.

TWOYZECK scrambles through the reeds, MARIE's body near him. The APPRENTICES watch him, hidden.

WOYZECK
The knife, the knife. Where's the knife? I left it here. It will give me away!

WOYZECK searches the reeds and water's edge.

WOYZECK
Warmer, warmer, warmer still? What kind of place is this? Something moved. Shhh, Franz. Quiet. Someone's here.

WOYZECK slinks through the reeds and trips over MARIE's body.

WOYZECK
Marie. Ha. Marie. So still, Marie. What made you so pale? Why have you got that red mark on your neck? What sins earned you that? You were black, Marie. Rotten with sin. Did I make you so pale? Why's your hair so wild? Didn't you have it in braids today? Haha! The knife, the knife!

WOYZECK pulls the knife from MARIE's body.

WOYZECK
There!

He runs to the water and lobs the knife into the pond.

WOYZECK
Goodbye knife! You'll sink like a stone in that water. Wait, no. Not there. That's too near the beach where they swim.

WOYZECK wades into the water. He retrieves the knife and throws it further.

WOYZECK
There! But no. In the summer, they dive after mussels? No, no, it'll rust soon enough. Unrecognizable. If only this heat had melted it.
WOYZECK catches a glimpse of his reflection in the water.

WOYZECK
I'm still bloody? I must wash. There's one stain. And there's another.

WOYZECK slowly, methodically scrubs his hands. As he continues, the cleaning devolves until he is dunking his head in the water, over and over, pushing his lungs to the limits of their capacity before coming up for air. In a ritual somewhere between a suicide by drowning and a baptism, WOYZECK continues this as his MOTHER and the CHILD enter MARIE's room and continues through MOTHER's story.

CHILD
Tell us a story, Grandma.

MOTHER
If you insist. Come now.

The CHILD settles into MOTHER's lap, much like WOYZECK had been settled into her lap earlier in the Inn.

MOTHER
Once upon a time, there was a poor child who had no mother and no father. Everything on earth was dead. And there wasn't a soul left. Everything was dead except this child. And the child wandered the world, searching. Night turned into day, day never turned to night, and the child never found anyone. So, the child decided, I shall go to Heaven. Surely there are people there. And indeed the moon still hovered above, happily providing some shadow from the sun. So the child built a great ladder and climbed all the way to the Moon. But when the child got there, the moon was just a hunk of rotten cheese. So the child headed towards the sun. But when they got there, the child found it was just a dying campfire. And all the stars nearby were just little flies, buzzing around the rotten body of the cosmos. So the child decided to go back to earth. But when they got there, they found out earth was just an overturned chamberpot. And the child was really all alone. So they sat there, alone and cried. And the child's still here to this very day, crying all alone.

END.

Made in the USA
Columbia, SC
26 April 2025